# Chatter in the Canopy

### Poems by Jeff Roberts

Drawings by
Dick Roberts & Doug Heinlein

ISBN: 1-4392-1481-6
ISBN-13:9781439214817
Library of Congress Control Number: 2008909362

Visit www.booksurge.com to order additional copies.

Thanks to the following publications in which these poems
originally appeared and to small presses everywhere – print
and virtual.

*Her Unusual Journey* was first published in the
Lawrence (Massachusetts) Eagle Tribune. It was first
published in book form in the Aurorean.

*The Rookery* was first published in the Lawrence
(Massachusetts) Eagle Tribune.

*Beach Glass* was first published in the Aurorean.

*Fish Story* was first published in Gotta Write #32.

*Manifesto* was first published in Recursive Angel.

*Refraction* was first published in ECTOPLASMIC
NECROPOLIS/Blood Pudding Press.

Thanks to the illustrators – Dick and Doug – for their
remarkable gifts and the chance to work together.

Thanks to Paul Haenel for years of thoughtful encouragement.

*For Barb*

# CONTENTS

# Tethers

Great Grandma haunts the stairs.
I heard her knee creak just now, and then
The tread stretch, as if that old wood
Would notice a ghost.

We hung a rope, as thick and smooth
As a ponytail, opposite the baluster,
So she could float –
Down the fanning risers –
Around the landing newel –
To the great room's foggy seascape
Clutching her cracked leather purse.

She shattered her hip when the dog
Pulled her off the porch by its leash
Chasing something reckless
That leans low into corners on two wheels.

# Badlands

My father is a fossil. Around him
Dawns flare. Dusks bleed.
The time between is Greek.

Oligocene: not much is new.

An inland sea shaved the buttes.
Today's faces all wear the same whiskers,
Making everything – so nothing – familiar.

In a photo taken when I was eight
He is bearded, wearing black-frame glasses
And a Hawaiian shirt. I'm sitting on his knee.

The gray peaks could be waves. No wonder
I'm lost. I may as well be traveling
The ocean between a man and his father.

*Poems by Jeff Roberts*

*Badlands – Richard J. Roberts*

# Alewives

They run at night when the stones are slick.

The net's long-handled pole lies across a hip,
Using the energy of sex against the water's push.

If the sport is conquest – a game of brain over fin
It will take a bucket filled to equal a trophy.

If the sport is supper – and soup is soup
Whether herring or shad – each dip
Fills as much stomach as a ladle.

Either way, the narrows glint silver and blue
Like a collection of antique letter openers.

Each fish slices through its windowed envelope
And is cashed as quickly as an unexpected check.

# Dry Clean Only

The suit is not wrinkled – it's rumpled.
Its furrows and five o'clock shadows
Need neither farmer nor steam. No matter
How carefully hung, attitude puckers the cuffs.

Attention to appearance can be a noble path.
Linen compliments a fat man. Tropical nights
Dab the sweat from your forehead when
Cool, dry women offer to help with your laundry.

# Evolution

The new thermostats chirp on and off
To tell the furnace to start or stop.

Remember the outrigger on the Pagsanjan
And the chatter in the canopy?

We linger under the morning covers
By choice now, not the fascism of frigid air.

We can be as lazy as the limp edges
Of quilt tucked under our chins.

Or—we can ride the sounds
Of monkeys in the morning.

*Evolution — Douglas D. Heinlein*

# Face Value
(for Paul Haenel)

I spent fifteen uncomfortable minutes
On the hopper in a unisex bathroom
Under a photograph captioned Lou Reed
And Laurie Anderson at the Hominy Grill.
Its thousand words—all questions.

Whose fifteen minutes were they?
Mine? The chef's? Lou and Laurie
Had theirs. (One expects the blank
Stare from Lou.) What does Laurie find
So amusing? My modesty? Shrimp

And grits for breakfast? Waking up
In South Carolina? What are they doing
In Charleston? Did they get soaked
Like me—walking up Meeting
Down Calhoun—right on Rutledge?

Answers don't come and—of course
A picture doesn't prove a thing
These days. Who can trust the eyes
Of a velvet Jesus? What miracle
Earned this space in such a chapel?

# The Rookery

In late October, a chill settles in the basement.
In the third floor bedroom, an antiqued-blue chest
At the foot of the bed becomes a nesting ground.

Several species of shorts winter here: cut-off denims,
Silk boxers, one-hundred-percent-cotton chinos.
Plaid baggies puff their pleats to scare interlopers.

Mating pairs entice each other with floppy pockets.
The shorts breed; they rear; they remain for months,
Fighting off wash-day trespassers, day-old underwear,

Wallets, wedgies, and wanderlust. In mid May,
When the Bakhtiari herd their goats back
Into the highlands; when the Pennacooks hike north

To Concord; when martins, swallows, terns, and warblers
Wing their way up coasts, the shorts tentatively explore
The second floor, testing the breezes, warming to travel.

# Moon Girls

This is the night I had in mind
When I built this deck. The night
To tilt a chair past its balance point
And catch myself against the rail.

The breeze dies mid-whisper
Taking the elm's rustle for a shush,
My cigarette for a librarian's finger.

It's here they say goodbye—from here
They call the cabs and fling the things
They think I treasure. It's here

I fish-mouth a smoke ring—and watch it
Milk its way through the watery sky
Rising on its own warm evil.

As it cheshires away, I recognize,
In its last curve, the full hip
Of one—on her way to the moon.

*Moon Girls — Douglas D. Heinlein*

# Helix Aspersa

No slime precedes its silent arrival,
Only rumors of slime—hard enough
To pave a victim's path.

Its vagabond bundle is slick
But dry, like shellac, and handsome
Deep mustard with mahogany stripe.

It leeches, from my memory, lazy hitches
Up to Maine, hoisting my own coiled pack
And battered cardboard lettered *North*
On one side, *Rockland* on the other.

It fields a foot
Where the stomach should be and ripples
The tacky callous, pulling itself over
The smooth pebbles like a tank, lumbering
Ass-backwards, up my coopered planter.

When eye to eye
It appears more cartoon than creature
Looping its tentacles in opposite orbits.

Thinking this its female side, I look for a strap
Or string in which to wedge a dollar
While she wiggles as slowly as Welk's baton.

In France, it would be hauled off as cargo:
Sixty to a pound, six to a serving.

In my garden, it finds its own way
Walking its walk, pacing its pace.

*Helix Aspersa — Richard J. Roberts*

# Her Unusual Journey

She never travels to where Polaris
Augers his flag and claims all around it
For the King of Winter. Nor will she visit
Where horses pull the wind.
Her warm airs annoy the mean temperatures.

She travels from the middle of somewhere and back
Spreading between degrees of mercury and latitude.

In Barrow, doors open no wider than a trash bag.
The caribou warm within the whisper of the pipeline.

Closer to home, the granite knuckles
Of my ancestors protrude from beneath the snow.
I feel her in my fingertips.
I hear her hum—and crack the lake like taffy.
Periscopes of crocus rise and mark
The bearings of her ship steaming north.
Her unusual journey begins in the middle
And ends where she turns, slapping her pockets
As if noticing forgotten keys
To retrace her obvious steps.

# Winnowing

Since you asked, I'll tell you why
Blueberries remind me of Sophia Loren.

It's because I was young once—in Maine
In summer—and worked a Tabbutt rake
Through sequins of low bush dew.

The sun made me think of a dark-haired girl
In a white apron with a baby crooked in one arm,
Her free hand sweeping damp hair
From her forehead—and I wanted to nurture.

I filled many bushels, and collected my pay.
Something fell to earth, and something blew away.

## manifesto

Angry young lizards
lounginNg in switzerland,
not really afraiD to take a stand
but feeling betteR about being part of a group.
staying up latE,

reading Breton's manifesto,
and dRawing corpses on tablecloths
after too much winE.
don't Tell us we've nothing to do.
hell, the kid in the cOrner is ubu roi's
graNdfather!

*Manifesto — Richard J. Roberts*

# Silent Bells
(for Kent)

Bells will herald welcome visitors
And pitchmen alike with no distinction.
Does Pisa's cold campanile announce
The presence of God or other gifts?

The moaning gong—the antiseptic
Echo of a chime—the surgical pealing
Of a siren—these are easy to heed
Or attend. What of the mute

And the broken? What of the silent
Knells—the subtle, small tinglings
That deliver news and warnings directly
To flesh without stinging the anvil?

Undiscovered wonders clamor between
The hammer blows. Does the tiny purple
Bellflower blast through a tenor—or toll
A suggestion by fingering the breeze?

*Silent Bells — Douglas D. Heinlein*

# Five-Mile River

In a hammock strung between buoys
She shifts her weight. The moon melts,
Greasing a path for the skiff.

Breath, no louder than a gull's wing, moves us
Past the marina, past Ginsberg's dock, then past
The black pilings speared into the muck.

Beyond the breakwater rougher seas
Pound against her hull. The friction of the wind
Heats the air between skull and scalp.

Who could sleep under a canvas of dead air?
The wheel spindles need only a familiar palm,
The throttle only a nudge; a boat, only a name.

*Five Mile River — Richard J. Roberts*

# The Nomad's Visitors

That kid Clifford—from first grade
In Ridgefield, (whose kid sister's
White angora pill-box skating cap still
Stiffens me in vivid REM-sleep)
Is here—in Racine, thumbing marbles
With a couple of kids my age
Who keep calling him Paul.

That ice-fishing shack—with tab "a"
Splintered into notch "c" (in which Denise
Snyder wrote *Let's kiss* in auger flakes
And licked her frozen finger, paralyzing me
For nearly an hour) is here—in Bethel
Jagged-edged and collapsing in a field
Behind our fifth house in eleven years.

That letter from my mother—typed because
She's sincere, and her chubby little scrawl
Is not (and which, had she written it sooner
Would have given me a chance to discover
Why Rachel Clark mutilated herself
With vicious men's dicks) is here—in Vienna
Waiting for words I'm afraid to invent.

# Oncology

You don't need to explain the irony
Of the positive shining like a negative—
The glow of a dark spot in cloudy film.

Let's say I agree—that your spot
Is like the moon and that whatever hangs
In a black sky is romantic—is there
To make us more comfortable with tenderness.

What if a spot—*What? No, any spot*—
Is ancient foxfire that will never reach us?

Okay—there really is a constellation
That includes your spot. By the time
Our eyes extend the crab's leg
To the scar on your tummy and back
It will be too late to carve a hole
In the sky and wonder about its breath.

# Black Hole

The absence of color has a name.
What name is the color of absence?

One can know something, as women do.
Or one can prove it, as some men do—
Viciously—carelessly—
Blaming the namers of colors
For compressing a world of matter
Into the size of a fist.

The infinite blackboard's equation of stars
Can name the color of missing teeth.

Then—with a name—
We can call it what it is.

*Black Hole — Douglas D. Heinlein*

# The Boatman

Every time the Boatman leans
Against his pole and pushes
The water's solid floor—the pole
Turns into a newspaper hat.

The canal is littered with old news

Like the bleeding gray dye of a cheap
Sweater in the wash. Should I try
Pushing a boat with a paper hat
Or is motion more personal than that?

*Poems by Jeff Roberts*

*The Boatman — Douglas D. Heinlein*

# Refraction

If you look away you can see
A pair of hands separate from their wrists
And know each part insists on equal truth.

You can watch ankles wave good-bye to their feet
And know neither is going away.

Knowledge, like love of anything
Is the water line that slices away
The things below and sets them adrift
In their own lighted shadows.

Where are the caramel shoulders
And the back as smooth and dark as a beetle's?

Stars misdirect with their subtle angles.
They hide right out in the open
In the places they just left.

Sometimes when you think a woman
Is upstairs reading, she's in the pool
Pillowed deep in that old air-raft
Dangling her arms in the water.

# Sleeping In

Some kids rise early but not this one.
Even when her father's icy lakes
Crackle like bacon frying
Her head of brambled anarchy
Stays nestled in his cool pillow.

A boy-dream blankets her
Settling in the low spots like fog.
This springald lingers. Breakfast brings
A new reproach for a too skimpy halter
Against the budding of April.

# Seduction

It's the sand in your voice that holds me.
That and the moonlight buttering your long ribs.

You can shout into the wind through cupped hands.
I can smell the salt and wet canvas.

What if I surrender to your rolling, black valleys—
To the tops of mountains kissed away?

When we collapse, flat-faced and ordinary,
On tar-colored foam and a dead skate—what then?

*Seduction — Richard J. Roberts*

# Titan

What sort of man's unhappy with the trees?
Perhaps this patch was never quite finished
And that is why my father's ill at ease
Until branches are stretched and varnished
To match some glossy pictures of perfection
Gleaned from teetering column caps
Of catalogs. The dogwood, upon inspection,
Wears locks, gussied with twine and bungee straps.
He squats on his deck, admiring the play
Of the breeze in the bracts, unaware
That one inch equals one foot—or of the way
The bonsai have lately missed their share
Of attention, to the benefit of giants that prevail
And promise the challenge of grander scale.

*Titan — Richard J. Roberts*

# There Never Was a Bird

There never was a bird—in that cage,
Whitewashed for company who never visit.
Never muss the unsoiled perch.
Never give a feather to the edge of the snipped wire.
Never enjoy the hole and its ocean view.

It is what it can be. It is an object
With a title. It is a prince among princes.
It is a cenotaph for soaring souls that fear delight.
It is a third image of the blue peninsula.
It is ekphrasis redux. It is connected *to* this *by* this.
It is *for* this that I am.

Her words were heavenly enough to name that cage.

If I could I would pin together the feathery paper scraps
Left behind—to build the poem named Object, Untitled.

Cornell, Joseph (1903-1972) *Towards the Blue Peninsula*
*(For Emily Dickinson)*
1953. 14.5 × 10.25 × 5.5 cm. Private Collection
Art © The Joseph and Robert Cornell Memorial Foundation/
Licensed by VAGA, New York, NY
Photo Credit: Edward Owen/Art Resource, NY
Used with permission

# Sadly, Our Geniuses Linger

(for Oscar Levant)

This witty suicide shtick is killer. I eat it up man.

You drink for free. The room comes with the gig.
Your ladder's got no bottom rung. Your keys don't fit nothin'.
Nothin' springs. Nothin' gets explored. You ain't checked out
Nothin' since them smoke-yellow tiles
slipped into the sky's clothing.

When you was movin' you plinked them keys. Now
Them fingers dig the rough pine leading up them seventeen steps
To your room. You memorize them everyday
On your way down. All you need to get home
Is to count seventeen. You walk like a sea horse man!
How d'you climb them steps anyway?

Every night ends with one long moan from the bottom
Of the scale. Ain't never true—never cathartic—only lazy.
That last note slides flat or straightens up just sharp enough
For pity to sing its only lyric. And I sing along. I applaud your style.
I listen. Each wire you rap shakes and wails its dirge. If you
Could stand you'd show me how to bend a note
'round my neck like silk. Instead you prop them chins
In your palm like you're marble and off center
Like some project out front of the library.

That Steinway gonna make a grand coffin—huge and dark
Like a yard of loam. That snifter gonna stand—a fitting but fragile
Stone. Wet rings gonna bleach the polish. They gonna circle
Places on that map for future crooners.

Forgotten squares leach the shapes of a hundred
Carbon fingernails into the edges of that classic lid
Leaving some fine filigree of frantic grasping.

# Fish Story

(for Ralph Hyle)

The bleed was the size of a dime.
As if there was a slot for a coin
In his skull, under the matted hair.

He forgets his kid's names.
He remembers the yellow spaniel
He took fishing in the forties.

At night, he's a broken lighthouse.
In the morning, I spill him
Into his wheelchair. Some mornings

I spill him again, out of the chair
Onto the slatted, redwood shower bench.
He cringes when I wash his crotch.

I lift his dead arm to rinse the pit.
He raises his good arm to illustrate
A tale about one that got away.

*Fish Story — Douglas D. Heinlein*

# Cold Shower

Without thinking I started
A trickle of hot water for shaving
As she showered. The little I took
Was instantly missed and chilled her
As careless words earlier
Had frozen the air between us.

In her cold mist—our awkward ritual
I soap her shoulders, hoping
The steam and friction will warm
The new words I choose to wash us.

# Sunrise, Sunset

The morning chores demand a naked light
Bold enough to penetrate the gauze
Grown thick around a swollen head of snooze.
To slide a blade through shadow shaves the night
And misses hair that needs to fall from grace
Or grow past death like Bradbury's wheat, each wail
From lack of scythe, a call for future toil.
Pity the pores once tweezed in dimmer place
Now scabbed and pocked by stabs in dawns gone by.
Lament the lip soon styptic dabbed, and damn
The twinge of surgery. Slickened chrome
Captures the warning of a sailor's sky.

Night's work requests a gentler radiance.
Details of the day need not be sharp. A smudge
Of toothpaste slugs a path across the bridge
It's made of my hairbrush handle's science.
A glass, splattered with ancient gargle, suggests
We remember the Prempro and Lipitor.
In the mirror I watch one candle's flare
Set in the bath, rouging your floating breasts.

# Cape Cod

A bare bulb porch light
Dangles above
A broken screen door
On a cottage in Chatham.

In the dull vanilla soft-serve glow
An old plastic bucket
Left behind on the stoop

Waits for morning
And the sounds
Of kids with little shovels
Full of sand.

*Cape Cod — Richard J. Roberts*

# Beach Glass
(for Anne Cowles Pinkney)

We could be the neck of a milk bottle
Or a bit of bobeche from a grand chandelier.

It doesn't matter what we were a part of
Before we were broken, only that we were

Broken and a part of something
And that our young edges were sharply fragile
And our translucence too common.

We know of waves, and still, now and then
Feel them vacuum the sand from beneath our feet
And pull us out and over and back, across the sand
As if we were something's great hobby
Tumbling in finer and finer and finer grit.

And it is the tumbling that matters
So much more than approval
Of combers or children, for if we have time
The tumbling will give us a texture
That transcends the standards
By which we are judged.

We remember so little
Of how the tumbling smoothed us
Only that, in the end, we are smooth.

## The Illustrators:

Richard J. Roberts (Dick) is Jeff's father. Dick is an artist, natural scientist, and historian and a life-long resident of Stamford, Connecticut where he has taken on the task of conducting a census of every gravesite in Stamford's cemeteries. Dick studied art with Delos Palmer in the 40's and in the 50s and 60's was the Curator of Exhibits at the Stamford Museum and Nature Center. Dick can be contacted through Jeff.

Douglas D. Heinlein (Doug) was Jeff's roommate in the army in the early 70's. Doug is the Academic Director for the Graphic Design and Interactive Media Design Departments at the Art Institute of Seattle. Doug is also an award-winning artist and designer with many years experience in the conceptualization, development and deployment of interactive media, multimedia and traditional design practices. His previous professional experiences include closerlook, inc., JamTV/Rolling Stone Network, and Imagination Pilots. He is the parent of two teenage boys and proud (as they claim) to be a worse influence than the Internet and TV combined. Add two cats (one deaf) and a big ole mutt. Shake, then pour. You can visit Doug's blog at http://47nx122w.blogspot.com

## Limited Edition Portfolios

50 portfolios of the 13 original drawings from this book with their poems are available. Each portfolio is numbered in pencil and signed by the author and both illustrators and is printed on 8.5 x 11 inch heavyweight, presentation matte paper with pigment-based ink. Please send inquiries to jeffrobertspoetry@gmail.com

Made in the USA
Columbia, SC
24 November 2024

46970887R00035